River Food Chains

Emma Lynch

www.heinemann.co.uk/library
Visit our website to find out more information about Heinemann Library books.

To order:
 Phone 44 (0) 1865 888066
 Send a fax to 44 (0) 1865 314091
 Visit the Heinemann Bookshop at www.heinemann.co.uk/library to browse our catalogue and order online.

First published in Great Britain by Heinemann Library, Halley Court, Jordan Hill, Oxford OX2 8EJ, part of Harcourt Education. Heinemann is a registered trademark of Harcourt Education Ltd.

Editorial: Sarah Eason and Kathy Peltan
Design: Jo Hinton-Malivoire and AMR
Picture Research: Ruth Blair and Ginny Stroud-Lewis
Illustration: Words and Publications
Production: Camilla Smith

Originated by Ambassador Litho Ltd
Printed in China by WKT Company Limited.

The paper used to print this book comes from sustainable resources

ISBN 0431 11900 7
09 08 07 06 05
10 9 8 7 6 5 4 3 2 1

British Library Cataloguing in Publication Data
Lynch, Emma
Food Chains: Rivers
577.6'416
A full catalogue record for this book is available from the British Library.

Acknowledgements
The Publishers would like to thank the following for permission to reproduce photographs: Ardea p. **17** (John Paul Ferrero); Corbis pp. **5** (David Muench), **10** (Adrian Arbib), **11** (Roger Wilmshurst; Frank Lane Picture Agency), **13** (Steve Austin/Papilio), **22** (Jeremy Horner), **26** (Layne Kennedy), **27** (Aaron Horowitz); Corbis/Webistan p. **24**; Heather Angel/Natural Visions pp. **7**, **12**, **18**; Nature Picture Library pp. **8** (Lynn M Stone), **14** (Niall Benuie), **16** (Anup Shah); NHPA p. **23**; Science Photo Library p. **25** (Mark Smith).

Cover photograph of a Nile crocodile reproduced with permission of NHPA / Martin Harvey.

The Publishers would like to thank Michael Scott for his assistance in the preparation of this book.

Disclaimer
All Internet addresses (URLs) given in this book were valid at the time of going to press. However, due to the dynamic nature of the Internet, some addresses may have changed, or sites may have changed or ceased to exist since publication. While the author and Publishers regret any inconvenience this may cause readers, no responsibility for any such changes can be accepted by either the author or the Publishers.

Every effort has been made to contact copyright holders of any material reproduced in this book. Any omissions will be rectified in subsequent printings if notice is given to the Publishers.

Contents

Words in bold, **like this**, are explained in the Glossary.

What is a river food web?

All living things are **organisms**. **Bacteria**, **algae**, plants, **fungi** and animals (including humans) are all organisms. Organisms are eaten by other organisms. Small animals get eaten by bigger animals which are eaten by even larger animals. When large animals die they get eaten by tiny insects, maggots and bacteria. Even mighty trees die and rot and are eaten by beetles, grubs and fungi. If you draw lines between each animal, showing who eats who, you create a diagram called a food web. It looks rather like a tangled spider's web!

The organisms in a river **habitat** are part of a food web. In food web diagrams, each arrow points from the food to the animal that eats it, from **prey** to **predator**.

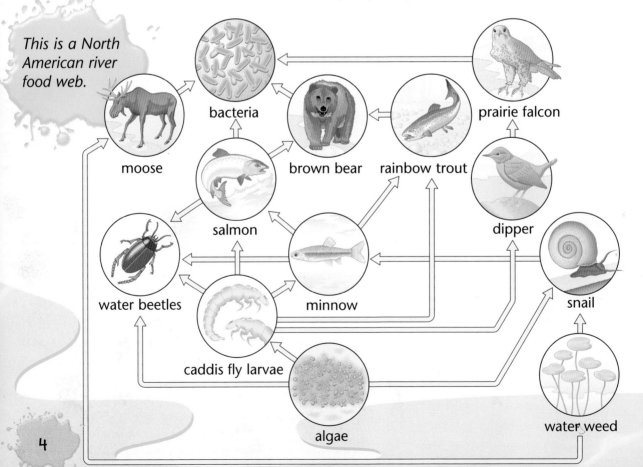

This is a North American river food web.

bacteria

prairie falcon

moose

brown bear   rainbow trout

salmon

dipper

water beetles

minnow

snail

caddis fly larvae

algae

water weed

4

What are river habitats like?

This book looks at the food web and food chains of river habitats. Rivers are large bodies of water that flow over land in a long channel. They are found all over the world. Some, like the Amazon River, cover huge distances (the Amazon is over 6400 kilometres/4000 miles long). Particular plants and animals live in river habitats because they are especially suited or **adapted** to life there. They are part of the river food web because the plants or animals they eat live in or around the river. Some, like fish, may live in the water. Some, like reeds and rushes, may grow along the river edges and banks. Some, like raccoons, may visit the river to look for food.

All rivers are home to a range of plants and animals that depend on each other for food and shelter.

What is a river food chain?

A food web looks quite complex, but it is actually made up of lots of different food chains. Food chains are simpler diagrams. They show the way some of the animals in a food web feed on each other. The arrows in the chain show the movement of food and **energy** from plants to animals as they feed on each other.

This is a North American river food chain. It shows how energy passes from one link in the chain to another.

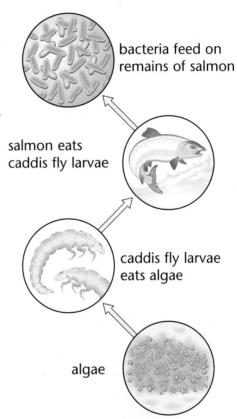

bacteria feed on remains of salmon

salmon eats caddis fly larvae

caddis fly larvae eats algae

algae

An **organism** can be part of more than one food chain if it eats more than one type of food, or if it is eaten by more than one hunter. Complex food webs, in which organisms eat more than one food type, are safer for the organisms within them. An organism that eats only one type of food will not survive if its food source disappears.

Starting the chain

Most food chains start with the energy that comes from the Sun. Plants trap the energy from sunlight in their leaves and use it to make their own food, in a process called **photosynthesis**.

Plants also take up **nutrients** from the soil through their roots and **carbon dioxide** from the air. Some river plants have roots into the mud on the river bed. Others float in or on the water. These may have little roots that hang in the water, or they may take in nutrients through their leaves. All plants use these nutrients, along with energy from food, to grow.

Every part of a plant can become food for animals in their **habitat**. They can eat the plant's roots, shoots, leaves, nuts, fruit, bark – or even the rotten plant when it has died. Without sunlight, all plants would die out. Then there would be no food for plant-eaters, and no plant-eaters for meat-eaters to eat, so most animals would die out too. Sunlight is at the beginning of all food chains, supplying the energy that is passed up the chain.

A plant's leaves are the factories where it makes food using energy from sunlight. The leaves grow in such a way as to catch the maximum amount of light.

Making the chain

Plants are called **producers**, because they trap the Sun's energy and produce food for other animals. Food chains usually start with plant producers. Producers provide food for plant-eating animals we call **herbivores**. In food chains we call these herbivores **primary consumers**. Primary consumers are often eaten by other animals we call **carnivores**. In food chains we call these carnivores **secondary consumers**. Secondary consumers catch and eat primary consumers, but they may also eat other secondary consumers. Animals that eat plants and other animals are called **omnivores**. Omnivores may be primary consumers or secondary consumers.

Raccoons are true omnivores – they eat fruit, wheat, corn, birds' eggs, insects and small river creatures such as this crayfish.

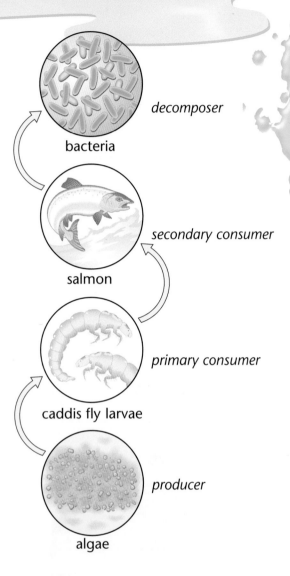

decomposer

bacteria

secondary consumer

salmon

primary consumer

caddis fly larvae

producer

algae

This food chain shows how energy passes from producer to consumers and decomposers.

More links in the chain

Food chains do not end when organisms die. First, **scavengers** such as worms and maggots eat their bodies. Then **decomposers** such as **bacteria** and **fungi** eat any dead remains that are left. The waste from these decomposers sinks into the soil or riverbed, where some of it becomes nutrients that can be absorbed by plant roots. In this way the chain begins again.

Breaking the chain

If some of the organisms in a food web die out, it may be disastrous for the others in the web. Sometimes natural events can damage a food web. **Droughts** may dry up a river, killing the animals and plants that live in water. The birds and animals that live around the riverbank, feeding on its plants, insects and fish, may also die. Human activity, such as **pollution** from farming and industry, can also cause breaks in river food chains and in natural cycles, with terrible results.

This river in the UK dried up during a drought, killing river plants and animals such as this crayfish.

Which producers live in rivers?

Plants are **producers** and they start most river food chains. There are many producers in a river **habitat**. Plants such as reeds and rushes grow along the river's banks. They provide places where water birds can build their nests. Water weeds grow in the river itself. In fast-flowing rivers, the broad leaves and white flowers of water crowfoot can be seen above the surface. Beneath the water the long stems lead down to roots growing deep into the river bed. These stop the plant being torn up by the strong current.

decomposer
bacteria

secondary consumer
salmon

primary consumer
caddis fly larvae

producer
algae

This bed of water crowfoot provides shelter for water snails, shrimps and insect *larvae*.

Microscopic, plant-like **algae** are also important river producers. They float in the water and are eaten by tiny creatures like water fleas. The fleas then become food for insects and small fish. Slimy algae grow on the rocks and pebbles at the river bottom, and are food for insects and water snails.

Water fleas are tiny relatives of shrimps and crayfish. They feed on algae, and are food themselves for some insect larvae and fish.

Breaking the chain: producers

Green plants are crucial to river food chains. In the 1960s, the Aswan **dam** was built to control the flow of the Nile River in Egypt. The dam has stopped the floods that every year brought rich **nutrients** to the fields around the river. Because the soil has become poorer, the Nile farmers now use chemical **fertilizers**. These chemicals drain from the fields into the river, and are **absorbed** by the plants. The Nile is also **polluted** from industry and by boats for tourists.

Much plant life on the Nile has died or been poisoned. Other animals in the food web, such as crocodiles and catfish, have died as a result. Work is under way to clean up the Nile and control the pollution, but the yearly floods will never come back.

Which primary consumers live in rivers?

River **primary consumers** are often **aquatic invertebrates** like freshwater shrimps, water lice, water beetles and insect **larvae**. The larvae of caddis flies live in rivers all over the world. They protect their soft bodies from **predators** by building a shell from sand, tiny twigs and even the empty shells of water snails. Most caddis fly larvae scrape **algae** off pebbles with their front legs to collect and eat, but some **species** also eat animals and are therefore **secondary consumers**.

Snails and other **molluscs**, such as river limpets also graze on water weeds and algae. Tadpoles nibble at plant matter in the first few weeks of their life, but when they get bigger they become secondary consumers and will also eat other small animals.

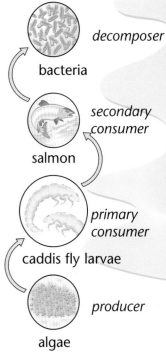

decomposer
bacteria

secondary consumer
salmon

primary consumer
caddis fly larvae

producer
algae

A caddis fly larva uses plant pieces or bits of gravel stuck to its shell as a disguise against predators.

Some primary consumers do not live under water. Water birds such as ducks swim on the surface, diving to the river bed to eat plants and algae. Water voles burrow long tunnels in the muddy riverbanks to hide from predators.

Larger consumers

Beavers are large **rodents** that build **dams** across rivers. With their huge teeth they gnaw down small trees to make their dams. The dams are usually about 25 metres (81 feet) long, but can be up to 500 metres (about 1640 feet)! The dam traps water, creating a deep, calm lake. In the middle of the lake the beavers build a wooden home called a lodge. Beavers eat bark, shoots and small saplings. They even keep a store of branches under water to eat in winter, when the lake ices over and they are trapped in their lodge.

Primary consumers can be very large. Moose wade in rivers to eat juicy water weed and escape biting flies. Where the Amazon meets the sea, manatees swim slowly along feeding on underwater plants. They can hold their breath for over 15 minutes.

This young water vole is feeding. Water voles nibble reeds, roots and shoots with their sharp teeth.

Which secondary consumers live in rivers?

Carnivores and omnivores are secondary consumers. Carnivores hunt other animals. Animals are rich in nutrients, but not always easy to catch, so carnivores use a lot of energy hunting their prey. The most common secondary consumers in rivers are fish. Small fish like bullheads lie at the bottom of the river beneath stones, waiting for fish fry or insects to swim by. Then they dart out and gobble them up with their large mouths. Bigger fish, such as salmon, sometimes hang almost motionless in the open river water, swimming against the current, waiting to grab larvae or insects that swim by.

Other common river carnivores are birds. Herons, bitterns and egrets hunt around the banks of slow-moving rivers. They stand motionless in the water, then quick as a flash they stab their beaks in the water and snap up small fish.

Larger carnivores also live in rivers. Otters have streamlined bodies, webbed feet and broad tails, which make them fast and agile swimmers. They eat fish, eels, crayfish, crabs and frogs. They will even raid birds' nests and eat the eggs or chicks.

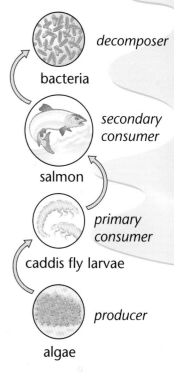

decomposer
bacteria

secondary consumer
salmon

primary consumer
caddis fly larvae

producer
algae

Breaking the chain: secondary consumers

The Amazon River in Brazil is under threat from habitat destruction. Illegal loggers are cutting down the forests around the river, destroying animal homes and sources of food. Animals like the giant otter are now highly endangered. The giant otter has also been hunted for its soft fur and is now nearly extinct.

In hot countries, huge carnivores like crocodiles and alligators sun themselves on the riverbanks. The huge Nile crocodile can grow to 6 metres (19 feet) long and can attack large prey like water buffalo. Few animals would dare attack an adult Nile crocodile, but their babies are often eaten by other large **reptiles**, such as the Nile monitor lizard.

Great herds of wildebeest move across the East African plains in search of fresh grass. When a herd crosses a river, it provides welcome food for crocodiles.

Omnivores hunt for prey, but will also eat plants. Brown bears visit rivers to catch fish, frogs or small **mammals**. They also look in the woods around the river for fruit, nuts, and small animals.

Which decomposers live in rivers?

When plants and animals die, **scavengers** and **decomposers** recycle the decaying matter into simpler substances, such as **carbon dioxide** and water. This releases **nutrients** back into the **habitat**, and provides plants with nutrients to grow, to convert the Sun's energy and start the chains and web again.

Many scavengers live at the bottom of the river, hiding in the shale or pebbles or in the soft river **silt** and mud. Some, like the crayfish, are **omnivores**. They eat rotting plants, dead fish, or even small, live animals. **Herbivores**, such as the ramshorn snail, graze on weeds and rotting leaves and stems.

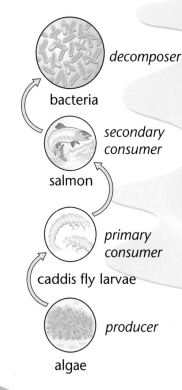

decomposer

bacteria

secondary consumer

salmon

primary consumer

caddis fly larvae

producer

algae

These shrimps eat the dead plants and animals that fall to the river bed.

Animals that die in the river can be attacked by **organisms** such as flatworms. Flatworms can sense rotting flesh a long way away. They find the decaying body and suck up its fluids with their long feeding tubes.

Flatworms eat dead plants as well as dead animals. This flatworm is on a decomposing leaf.

Decomposers such as **bacteria** and **fungi** break down dead organisms until they rot and dissolve. Some of the dissolved nutrients fall to the bottom of the river. Many are carried away by the current in fast-flowing rivers. The nutrients are carried a long way, to the slower parts of the river. Slower parts of rivers often have muddier water and more animal life because the water is thick with nutrients.

How are river food chains different in different places?

Food chains can be very different from one river to another, or even along the length of one river. They are affected by **climate**, the speed and depth of the water, and human activity.

The River Nile

The Nile is the world's longest river, at about 6650 kilometres (4132 miles). It starts in the mountains of central Africa, and as it reaches flatter land it runs through deserts and swamps to the vast Nile Delta, where it flows into the Mediterranean.

The thick roots of tall papyrus reeds slow down parts of the river, creating a swamp where hippos wallow. Pied kingfishers watch the river from the papyrus, then dive down into the water to catch small fish.

Nile water shrews are common along the riverbanks. They are **prey** for the enormous Nile perch. Smaller fish are caught by fish eagles that swoop down from the sky. Nile crocodiles hunt the perch and other fish, including the catfish that turn upside down to feed on surface plants.

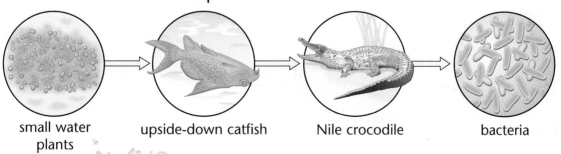

small water plants → upside-down catfish → Nile crocodile → bacteria

This is a Nile river food chain.

The Missouri–Mississippi River

The Missouri–Mississippi River is the fourth largest river in the world. The Missouri and the Mississippi flow through the grasslands and marshlands of central America until they meet to form one mighty river. The river slows down, flooding its banks and forming areas of swampland until it finally enters the sea.

The slow, **nutrient**-rich river is ideal for plantlife, and among the plants live thousands of crayfish. They feed on insects, snails, tadpoles and rotting plants and animals. They are preyed upon by large **salamanders** called mudpuppies. Mudpuppies make a nice snack for the blue catfish, which can grow up to 1.5 metres long. Small catfish are in turn at risk from the great blue heron.

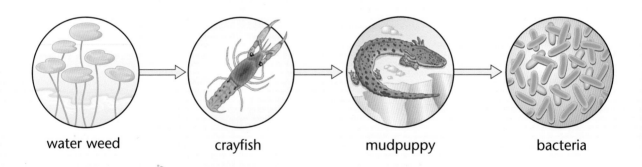

water weed   crayfish   mudpuppy   bacteria

This is a Missouri–Mississippi River food chain.

The Amazon River

This South American river is the mightiest of all rivers. Every year in the rainy season it gets even bigger, fed by the rains and melting water from the mountains, and breaks its banks. Nutrient-rich water floods the land for miles around, watering the Amazonian rainforest.

There are more **organisms** here than anywhere else on Earth. Lush plants grow along the banks and floodplains, forming forests and grasslands. The world's largest **rodent**, the 1 metre-long capybara, lives here, hunted by caimans and by anacondas.

The river supports up to 3000 different **species** of fish, including the world's largest freshwater fish, the arapaima. Tiny daphnia are eaten by angel fish. Their flat shape makes it easy for angel fish to hide in the weeds. Razor-toothed piranhas can strip a dead capybara down to the bone in less than one minute! They are **scavengers** and **predators**.

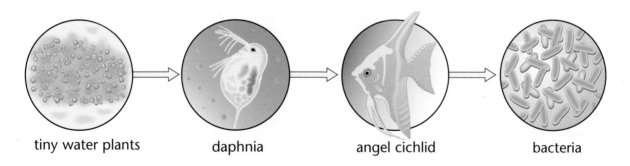

tiny water plants   daphnia   angel cichlid   bacteria

This is an Amazon River food chain.

What happens to a food web when a food chain breaks down?

All over the world, river food chains and webs are under threat because of humans. Although much work is under way to stop the damage, these are some of the dangers currently faced by plants and animals in river **habitats**.

Pollution

The Nile and the Ganges rivers are severely **polluted** by chemicals from industry, farming and domestic waste. These poison the plants and animals, reducing their numbers or driving them away from their natural habitat.

The Ganges river is a holy river for Hindus, and thousands bathe in it each day, but its waters are dangerously polluted with sewage.

Habitat destruction

The Amazon rainforest is being destroyed as trees are cut down. This **logging** is destroying the habitat for wildlife. Animal numbers are declining as there is less cover for **prey** to hide from **predators**. Without trees along the riverbank, there is less shade for river animals and fewer leaves fall into the river as food for the fish there.

The spectacled caiman catches pirahna fish and other prey along the banks of the Amazon River.

Overhunting

Animals of the Amazon River are at risk from overfishing and overhunting. The giant otter, spectacled caiman and red-headed turtle are all **endangered** animals, hunted almost to **extinction** for their fur, skin or meat. Unless they are protected they will be gone for ever.

Dams

On the Missouri and Nile rivers **dams** control how much water flows down them throughout the year. This limits the floods that damage industry, but many river **species** rely on the natural way the water rises and falls during the year. On the Missouri, pallid sturgeon need high water flow to **spawn**, while least terns and piping plovers need low flow so they can nest on the banks. The numbers of all these animals have fallen in recent years, but there are now plans to make the dams mimic some of the natural flows of the river.

The Nile river is choked with water hyacinths. In some places weevils (a type of beetle) released among the hyacinth beds have controlled their spread.

Breaking the chain: unwanted additions

Food chains can be broken if we introduce a new **organism** to a habitat. For example, in the 1800s travellers brought the water hyacinth to Africa, from the Amazon. It was not part of the natural diet of any Nile animals, and spread quickly. The water hyacinth can double its weight in twelve days, and grows faster than mechanical cutters can clear it. It has now spread to most of Africa's lakes and rivers. The huge mats it forms prevent light and oxygen reaching life beneath the river's surface, which reduces the variety of fish in the river. Water hyacinth affects fishing, water supplies, shipping and power generation.

How can we protect river food chains?

All around the world, scientists, **environmental** groups and governments are working to clean up and protect rivers and river food chains.

International research and protection

Scientists conduct surveys into river **habitats**. They test water quality and **pollution** levels and they monitor animal and plant life around rivers to ensure that population levels do not fall. In this way scientists discover the links in the food web that need protection.

In the Amazon, scientists have discovered that gold mining and farming in the Andes mountains may be damaging fish **spawning** grounds. The fish **fry** that hatch here **migrate** along the Amazon River. Destruction of these spawning grounds would destroy adult fish life thousands of miles downstream.

The tambaqui is a fish that lives in the Amazon River. It feeds on fruit and nuts that fall into the river.

Washing machines, refrigerators, barrels and tyres are among the huge piles of rubbish removed from the Mississippi by conservation workers.

Scientists make recommendations to governments about how they can improve and protect river habitats, both for the wildlife and for the people who live along the river. Around the Missouri–Mississippi, laws have been passed to stop the use of some harmful chemicals in farming. Environmental groups, like Friends of the Earth, Greenpeace and WWF, **campaign** to ensure that governments look after rivers and to make the public aware of the problems. They try to prevent pollution from industry and farming and illegal **logging** near rivers, and suggest alternative ways of managing rivers where **dams** are threatening wildlife.

Conservation groups also run projects to educate people living near rivers, to raise their awareness of how they can help to protect them for everyone's future.

Research a river food web in your local area

You can research river habitats in your area. If you go on a trip near a pond or river, think about the food chains there. Here are some suggestions to help you find out about animal and plant life and some tips to help you protect the environment.

1. What is the habitat like? Is it cold, warm, shady, light?
2. Can you see any plants or animals? Try to group them – which are the plants, insects, birds, fish and **amphibians**?
3. What do you think each animal would like to eat?
4. Which are the **predators** and which are the **prey**?
5. Can you make a food chain of the animals and plants you see?
6. Think about how the habitat could change – how would it affect the wildlife?
7. Is there evidence of pollution or habitat destruction?

We would all like to live near unpolluted rivers like this one. But even rivers in busy cities can be healthy habitats for animals and plants if people work to keep them free of pollution and rubbish.

27

Where are the world's main rivers?

This map shows the location of some of the world's biggest rivers.

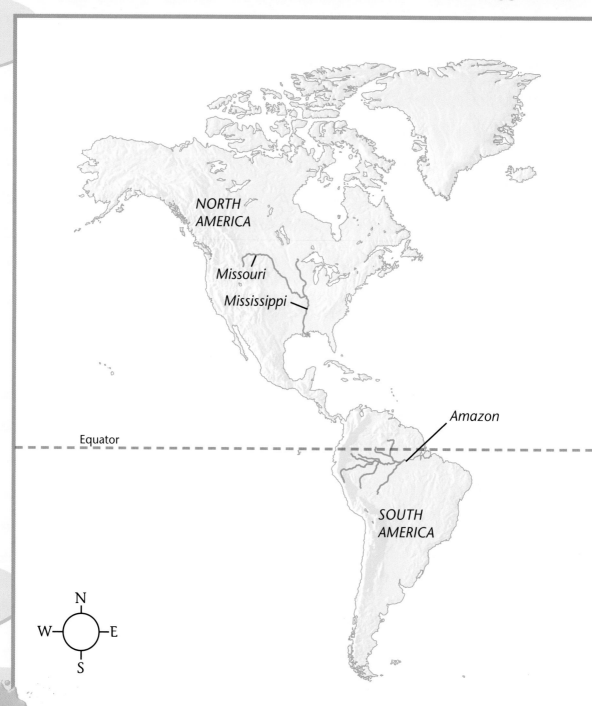

NORTH
AMERICA

Missouri

Mississippi

Amazon

Equator

SOUTH
AMERICA

N
W—E
S

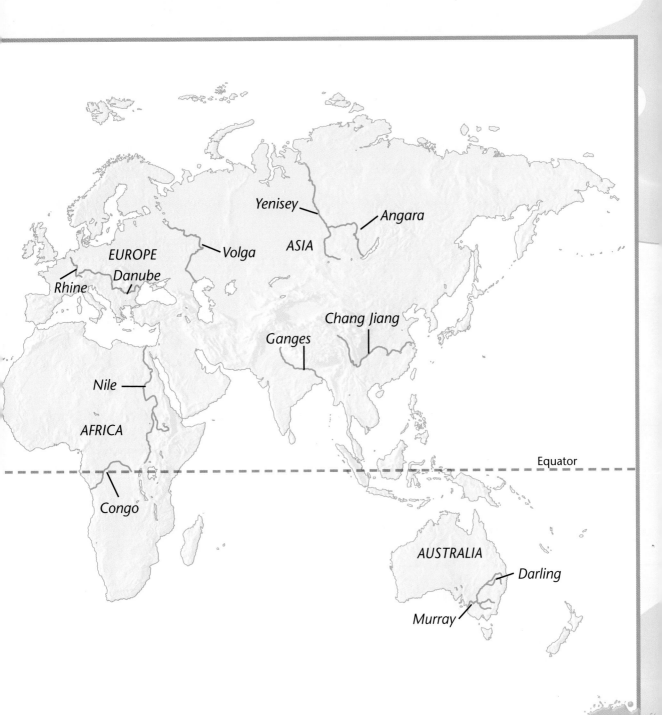

Glossary

absorb take in through the surface of skin, leaves or roots

adapt change in order to survive better in a particular place

algae (singular alga) small plant-like organisms

amphibians group of animals that breed in water but live part of their life on land

aquatic living in water

bacteria (singular bacterium) tiny living decomposers found everywhere

campaign work to get something done or changed

carbon dioxide gas in the air which animals breathe out and plants use to make food

carnivore animal that eats the flesh of another animal

climate the general conditions of weather in any area

conservation protecting and saving the natural environment

consumers organisms that eat other organisms

dam structure built across a river to stop water that would otherwise flow along the river

decomposers organisms that break down and get nutrients from dead plants and animals and their waste

drought a long period with no rain

endangered when a species of animal or plant is in danger of dying out completely

energy power to grow, move and do things

environment the surroundings in which an animal or plant lives, including the other animals and plants that live there

extinct when a species has died out completely

fertilizers substances that are sprayed on to land to make crops grow better

fry young fish

fungi group of decomposer organisms including mushrooms, toadstools and their relatives

habitat place where an organism lives

herbivore animal that eats plants

invertebrate animal without a backbone

larvae (singular larva) the young of some insects and other animals

logging chopping down trees

mammals group of animals that feed their babies on milk from their own bodies

migrate move to another place for part of the year, then back again

molluscs soft-bodied animals, often with hard shells, such as snails, oysters and octopuses

nutrients chemicals that plants and animals need to live

omnivore animal that eats both plants and other animals

organism living thing

photosynthesis process by which plants make their own food from carbon dioxide, water and energy from sunlight

pollution when chemicals or other substances that can damage animal or plant life escape into soil, water or the air

predator animal that hunts and eats other animals

prey animals that are caught and eaten by predators

primary consumer animal that eats plants

producer organism (plant) that can make its own food

reptile cold-blooded animal covered in scales

rodent mammal with large gnawing front teeth, such as a mouse or rat

salamander amphibian shaped like a lizard

scavengers organisms that feed on dead plants and animals and waste

secondary consumers animals that eat primary consumers and other secondary consumers

sewage waste carried away in the drains

silt tiny pieces of rock and mud that settle at the bottom of a river

spawn produce its young as eggs

species group of organisms that are very similar and can breed together to produce young

Find out more

Books and CD-Roms

Cycles in Nature: Food Chains, Theresa Greenaway (Hodder Wayland/Raintree Steck–Vaughn, 2001)

Science Answers: Food Chains and Webs, Louise and Richard Spilsbury (Heinemann Library, 2004)

Taking Action: WWF, Louise Spilsbury (Heinemann Library, 2000)

Food Chains and Webs CD-ROM (Heinemann Library, 2004) has supporting interactive activities and video clips.

Websites

www.yahooligans.yahoo.com/content/science/movies/foodchains.html
www.enchantedlearning.com/biomes
These sites have films, games and information about river food chains.

Find out more about the conservation work of these organizations at:

www.wwf.org.uk   WWF-UK
www.wwf.org.au   WWF Australia
www.foe.co.uk   Friends of the Earth UK
www.foe.org.au   Friends of the Earth Australia

Index

Titles in the *Food Chains and Webs* series include:

Hardback   0 431 11903 1

Hardback   0 431 11905 8

Hardback   0 431 11904 X

Hardback   0 431 11902 3

Hardback   0 431 11901 5

Hardback   0 431 11900 7

Find out about the other titles in this series on our website www.heinemann.co.uk/library